EARTH'S NATURAL BIOMES

MARINE BIOMES

Louise and Richard Spilsbury

WAYLAND
www.waylandbooks.co.uk

Published in paperback in Great Britain in 2019 by Wayland

Copyright © Hodder and Stoughton, 2017

All rights reserved

Editor: Hayley Fairhead
Design: Smart Design Studio
Map (page 6) by Stefan Chabluk

ISBN: 978 1 5263 0132 1
10 9 8 7 6 5 4 3 2 1

MIX
Paper from responsible sources
FSC® C104740

Wayland, an imprint of
Hachette Children's Group
Part of Hodder and Stoughton
Carmelite House
50 Victoria Embankment
London EC4Y 0DZ

An Hachette UK Company
www.hachette.co.uk
www.hachettechildrens.co.uk

Printed and bound in China

All photographs supplied by Nature Picture Library
www.naturepl.com

Front cover(main), title page(b) and p9 Aflo; title page(main) and p28 Michael Pitts; p4 Wim van den Heever; p5 Tui De Roy; p6, front cover(tr) and title page(tr) Klein and Hubert; p7 and contents page(t) Alex Mustard; p8 Jeff Rotman; p10 Georgette Douwma; p11 Laurie Campbell; p12, front cover(br) and contents page(b) Pascal Kobeh; p13 and back cover(tr) Alex Mustard; p14 and p32(b) Roy Mangersnes; p15 Doug Allan; p16 David Shale; p17 Doug Perrine; p18 Franco Banfi; p19 and p31(b) Chris and Monique Fallows; p20 Alex Mustard; p21 and imprint page(t) Pedro Narra; p22 Solvin Zankl / Geomar; p23 and imprint page(b) Tom Mangelsen; p24 and p31(t) Franco Banfi; p25 and back cover(tl) Jose B. Ruiz; p26, front cover(tl) and p32(t) Roland Seitre; p27 Dan Barton; p29 Brandon Cole.

Every attempt has been made to clear copyright. Should there be any inadvertent omission, please apply to the publisher for rectification.

The website addresses (URLs) included in this book were valid at the time of going to press. However, it is possible that contents or addresses may have changed since the publication of this book. No responsibility for any such changes can be accepted by either the author or the Publisher.

CONTENTS

What are marine biomes? 4
Marine biomes of the world 6
Living underwater 8
Coasts 10
Coral reefs 12
Frozen oceans 14
In the deep 16
Ocean predators 18
Born survivors 20
Eat or be eaten 22
Oceans and people 24
Marine threats 26
Marine futures 28
Glossary 30
Find out more 31
Index 32

WHAT ARE MARINE BIOMES?

Marine biomes cover about three-quarters of the Earth's surface. They include open ocean water, the world's coastlines and seashores, colourful coral reefs, the mysterious hidden world of the deep, dark oceans and the seabed.

Ocean challenges

Marine biomes are challenging places for plants and animals to live. The salt in seawater would dry out and kill most living things if they drank a lot of it. Winds across the water's surface whip up high waves that can be rough and powerful. In places, oceans reach incredible depths and the deeper it gets the darker and colder it becomes.

Marine biomes are home to many different animals, such as these bottlenose dolphins surfing high waves in waters off South Africa.

Amazing Adaptation

Adaptations are special features or body parts that living things develop over time to help them survive in a biome. Sea lions and dolphins have strong, paddle-like flippers to help them swim and a long, narrow body shape to cut through waves.

Ocean survival

In spite of these challenges the marine biome is full of life. Plankton consists of tiny plants so small they cannot be seen without a microscope, but there can be over a million plankton in just a litre of seawater! In contrast, some types of seaweed can be up to 30 metres long.

There is a huge variety of marine animals, too. Some, such as fish, live, breathe, feed and have their young in the oceans without ever leaving the water. Others, including the millions of sea birds that fly over the water searching for fish, only visit the ocean biome to catch food.

Some animals, such as sea lions, live mainly in seawater but come to the surface to breathe or go ashore to rest and have their young.

Fact Focus: Biome or Habitat?

Biomes are regions of the world that have a similar climate, plants and animals, such as deserts, forests, rivers, oceans, tundra and grassland. A habitat is the specific place in a biome where a plant or animal lives.

MARINE BIOMES OF THE WORLD

There are five oceans in the world but they are all connected and water flows between them. Within these marine biomes there are also seas, smaller areas of an ocean that are usually partly surrounded by land.

The Arctic Ocean

The Arctic covers the area around the North Pole. This ocean is the smallest in the world. It is so cold that its centre is permanently covered with ice three metres thick. In summer, the edges of the ocean melt.

The Southern Ocean

The Southern, or Antarctic Ocean, surrounds the continent of Antarctica. In winter, the water around the edges of Antarctica freezes. In summer, this melts again. It has several seas, including the huge Weddell Sea.

Adelie penguins dive off Antarctic ice into the Southern Ocean to catch food, such as shrimp-like krill (see page 22).

The oceans are mostly divided up by the seven continents, except for the Southern Ocean which runs into other oceans.

The Indian Ocean

The Indian Ocean is the warmest on Earth because a large part of it lies in the tropics. Some of the Indian Ocean's surface water is as hot as a warm bath!

The Atlantic Ocean

The Atlantic Ocean is the second largest ocean on Earth. It is warmer near the Equator and colder in the far north and south. The Atlantic contains seas, such as the North Sea and the Caribbean Sea.

The Pacific Ocean

The Pacific Ocean is the biggest of the five oceans. Where it meets the Southern Ocean, its waters are freezing cold, but near the Equator, its waters are much warmer.

Amazing Adaptation

The hammerhead shark's eyes are at the ends of its hammer-shaped head so it can see all around when looking for prey.

Hammerhead sharks live in the Pacific, Atlantic and the Indian Oceans.

LIVING UNDERWATER

Living underwater is hard work! Two major challenges facing living things are finding oxygen to breathe underwater and the problem of drinking salty seawater.

Breathing

Seaweed, a plant-like algae growing in marine biomes, releases a gas called oxygen into seawater as part of photosynthesis. Most living things need to take in oxygen to survive. Fish breathe underwater by using their gills. Some fish gulp water into their mouth and pump it over the gills. Oxygen dissolved in seawater passes into the gills and the fish's body. Other fish force water past their gills as they swim forwards with their mouths open.

The sand tiger shark has five large gill slits on each side of its pointed head. It can breathe while still or moving.

Surviving the salt

Some marine animals, such as sea otters, have extra-large kidneys. These body parts work hard to remove the salt from seawater and get rid of it in the animal's urine. The sea turtle empties salt from its body through its eyes — and looks like it's crying as it does so!

On the move

Friction between the water and its body can slow an animal down. That's why many marine animals are a long, narrow, streamlined shape. This reduces the area at the front of their body pushing against the water, so they can move more quickly. Fish, dolphins and whales move their tails up and down to swim and dive. Fins help them to steer, brake and balance. Some animals have flippers or webbed feet to push against the water.

Other animals move by jet propulsion! Octopus, squid and some jellyfish open out the bell-shaped top part of their body and fill it with water. Then they squeeze it tight to push the water out. The push of the water moves them forwards.

As a sea nettle jellyfish swims along, its long tentacles stun fish and other prey that brush against it. The tentacles then drag prey into its mouth.

Amazing Adaptation

Most fish have a gas-filled bag called a swim bladder just below their backbone. The swim bladder fills with air to help fish float and releases air so fish can sink and dive.

COASTS

Coasts are constantly changing. Powerful waves crash into the land and rising and falling tides cover a shore with seawater, then expose it to harsh wind and hot sun.

Super seaweed

A large breaking wave is strong enough to shift rocks and move piles of sand along a beach. The rubbery types of seaweed that live near the coast have parts called holdfasts that hold them tightly to rocks. They also have leaf-like parts called fronds that are flexible and bend with the waves, so they don't get broken as they float in the water. Many seaweeds are covered in slime that stops them drying out when the tide goes out.

Amazing Adaptation

Many types of seaweed have air-filled pockets along their fronds that help them float near the surface. This allows them to capture sunlight energy they use to make food in a process called photosynthesis.

Kelp is a giant seaweed that can form large underwater forests. It has huge holdfasts to anchor it to the ocean floor.

Saved by the shell

The soft bodies of many coastal animals are covered in shells. Molluscs, such as limpets and barnacles, have a muscular foot that sucks tightly onto rocks. They hide beneath hard, cone-shaped shells so waves don't wash them away. At low tide, their shells stop the sun and wind drying them out. Hard shells also protect animals, such as crabs, from some of the birds, fish and other predators that try to eat them.

Hide and seek

Another way to escape harsh winds, drying sun, strong waves and predators is to hide under the sand! Sand mason worms are about 30 centimetres long. They live under the sand but build a tube out of bits of shell, mud and sand cemented together with mucus, or spit, above the surface. They use the tube to keep safe when they come out of the sand to capture plankton from the water to eat.

Tentacles

A sand mason worm captures food using tentacles that sprout from its head. The top of the tube is shaped to support the finger-like tentacles when they are stretched out.

CORAL REEFS

Coral reefs are the most colourful habitats in the marine biome. These rocky structures form in fairly shallow water in warm oceans and provide food and shelter to many different animals. They can be enormous, but they are built by tiny creatures called coral polyps.

Amazing Adaptation

Giant moray eels are about three metres long and have long, thin bodies they can squeeze into cracks in the reef. They hide here until they smell prey. Then they dart out and ambush it.

Coral construction

Coral polyps are like tiny, soft-bodied animals. They take calcium from seawater to help them build cup-shaped cases of limestone to protect their soft bodies. Over time, thousands of these stony cases grow together to form coral reefs. The polyps living inside only stretch out their tiny tentacles to feed at night. Plant-like algae live among corals as well as animals, such as starfish and moray eels.

Moray eels come out of their coral reef caves to grab slippery prey, such as fish and octopus, in their large, sharp teeth.

Fishing on the reefs

Parrotfish teeth are fused together to form a sort of beak that can chip off pieces of coral to eat. Angelfish have long snouts and sharp teeth that they poke into small gaps to graze on the algae there.

A clownfish has a unique relationship with sea anemones. Sea anemones live in one place and catch small shrimp and fish with their poisonous tentacles. A clownfish is too big for the anemone to eat and is unaffected by the anemone's deadly stings. It lives among the tentacles, safe from predators and feeds on damaged tentacles and tiny animals that could harm the anemone.

> The sea anemone provides safe shelter for the clownfish which in turn protects the sea anemone from pests.

Fact File: The Great Barrier Reef

Location: North-east coast of Australia
Size: Over 2,000 kilometres long
Overview: The biggest coral reef in the world — it can be seen from the moon! It has many different coloured corals and animals, such as sea turtles and dolphins.

FROZEN OCEANS

Few animals can survive the icy oceans near the North and South Poles. The water here is bitterly cold and it's often frozen into a layer of solid ice at the surface. Algae grow on the underside of the ice and in summer a lot of plant plankton floats in the water.

The bearded seal uses its webbed feet like paddles to push against the water and help it swim along.

Bearded seals

Bearded seals, like polar bears and Adelie penguins, have dense waterproof fur and a thick layer of fat, called blubber, under their skin to keep warm in Arctic waters. Bearded seals dive to feed on the ocean floor under sheets of ice, but return to the surface to breathe. They use their hard heads to crash through thin ice to create breathing holes.

Amazing Adaptation

The bearded seal has good hearing to help it detect the tiny noises made by animals on the ocean floor and large eyes to see fish, such as Arctic cod, swimming in dimly-lit waters. It gets its name from the long, white, drooping whiskers on its face. These sensitive whiskers help it to feel around the ocean floor for crabs and shellfish to eat.

Ice fish

Some fish in the Southern Ocean survive by living deep in its waters, because here the water stays at a more constant temperature and does not freeze. Ice fish are one of the few types of fish that can live their whole lives in these icy waters. Their secret is their ability to make substances, nicknamed antifreeze, in their blood, which lower the point at which the body freezes. It stops ice growing inside the fish's body.

The ghostly-looking blackfin ice fish has a large mouth with small teeth for grasping fish, crabs and other prey that it catches near the ocean floor.

Fact Focus: Life in the Slow Lane

Most of the animals that live in frozen oceans live longer than similar animals in other oceans. The reason is that the cold temperatures slow everything down so animals do everything at a much gentler pace, using less energy.

IN THE DEEP

A little light still reaches the ocean around 50 m below the ocean's surface, but 600 m down it is pitch-black and there are some strange and fearsome looking animals.

Deep-sea anglers

Deep-sea animals have developed some amazing ways of catching prey in the darkness. Some fish, octopus and squid have parts called photophores on their body. These contain bacteria that can produce light. Angler fish get their name from a spine that dangles a photophore (a body part that produces light) near their mouth. They wave this to and fro like a fishing pole to attract prey. When a fish gets close enough, the angler fish snatches it up in its needle-sharp teeth.

Amazing Adaptation

An angler fish can stretch its jaw and stomach to swallow prey twice the size of its body. This allows it to stock up on food when it can, because there are fewer fish to prey on in the deep sea.

An angler fish has teeth which are anlged inwards, so its prey cannot escape once caught.

Deep-sea divers

Sperm whales dive as deep as 1,000 m hunting for prey, such as giant squid. To find prey in deep ocean waters where it is too dark to see, they use echolocation. First, they make and send out high-pitched sounds. These spread out in the water and when they hit an animal, such as a squid, the sounds reflect or bounce back towards the whale.

The whale can find out where the prey is and how big it is by working out where the echoes come from and how long it takes for them to return.

Sperm whales hold their breath for up to 90 minutes when diving. Their 20-cm-long teeth weigh up to 1 kilogram each and help them to eat about 1,000 kg of fish and squid a day!

Fact File: The Mariana Trench

Location: The western Pacific Ocean
Size: 2,540 km long and 70 km wide at widest point and 11,000 m below sea level
Overview: The deepest point on Earth, this trench on the sea floor is deeper than Mount Everest is high.

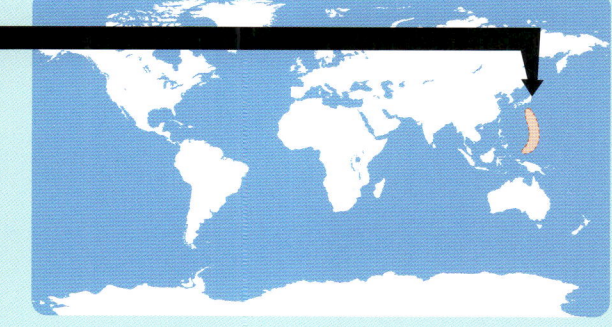

OCEAN PREDATORS

The ocean is a dangerous place where deadly predators use a variety of tactics to catch and eat other animals in the battle for survival.

Red demons

Humboldt or jumbo squid are nicknamed red demons because they have photophores that rapidly change the appearance of their skin to red while they are hunting. Amazingly they use the red colour as camouflage to help them catch prey: sunlight is made up of different colours and red light is weak and cannot reach far underwater, so red animals look black and are hard to see.

Each of the jumbo squid's eight, long tentacle arms has about 100-200 suckers along it and each sucker is lined with more than 20 razor-sharp teeth. The suckers drag prey towards the squid's large, sharp beak so it can eat them.

A jumbo squid uses its tentacles as deadly weapons to catch another squid.

Fact Focus: Hide and Seek

Many marine animals use camouflage to hide from predators. Flatfish are shaped like plates. Many are brown and speckled and are impossible to see when lying flat on the sand.

Clever colouration

Many fish, whales and dolphins have a dark back and a light belly. This is called countershading. When animals swimming below them look up, the light colour of the belly blends in with light shining into the ocean from above. When animals swimming above them look down, their dark back blends in with the darkness below. Some prey animals use countershading to hide. Great white sharks use it as camouflage to sneak up on prey!

Amazing Adaptation

When sharks lose teeth in an attack they simply regrow them. A shark may lose and grow up to 30,000 teeth in its lifetime.

Great white sharks

A great white shark attack is sudden and vicious. The shark moves its tail fin side to side quickly to shoot up through the water. As it nears the surface it opens its mouth to snatch up prey as it bursts through the surface. It often kills prey with one huge bite.

The great white shark's huge mouth is full of razor-sharp teeth that can bite through skin, flesh and bone of prey, such as seals, squid and dolphins.

BORN SURVIVORS

Some ocean animals have amazing ways to make sure their eggs or young get the best start in life in the marine biome.

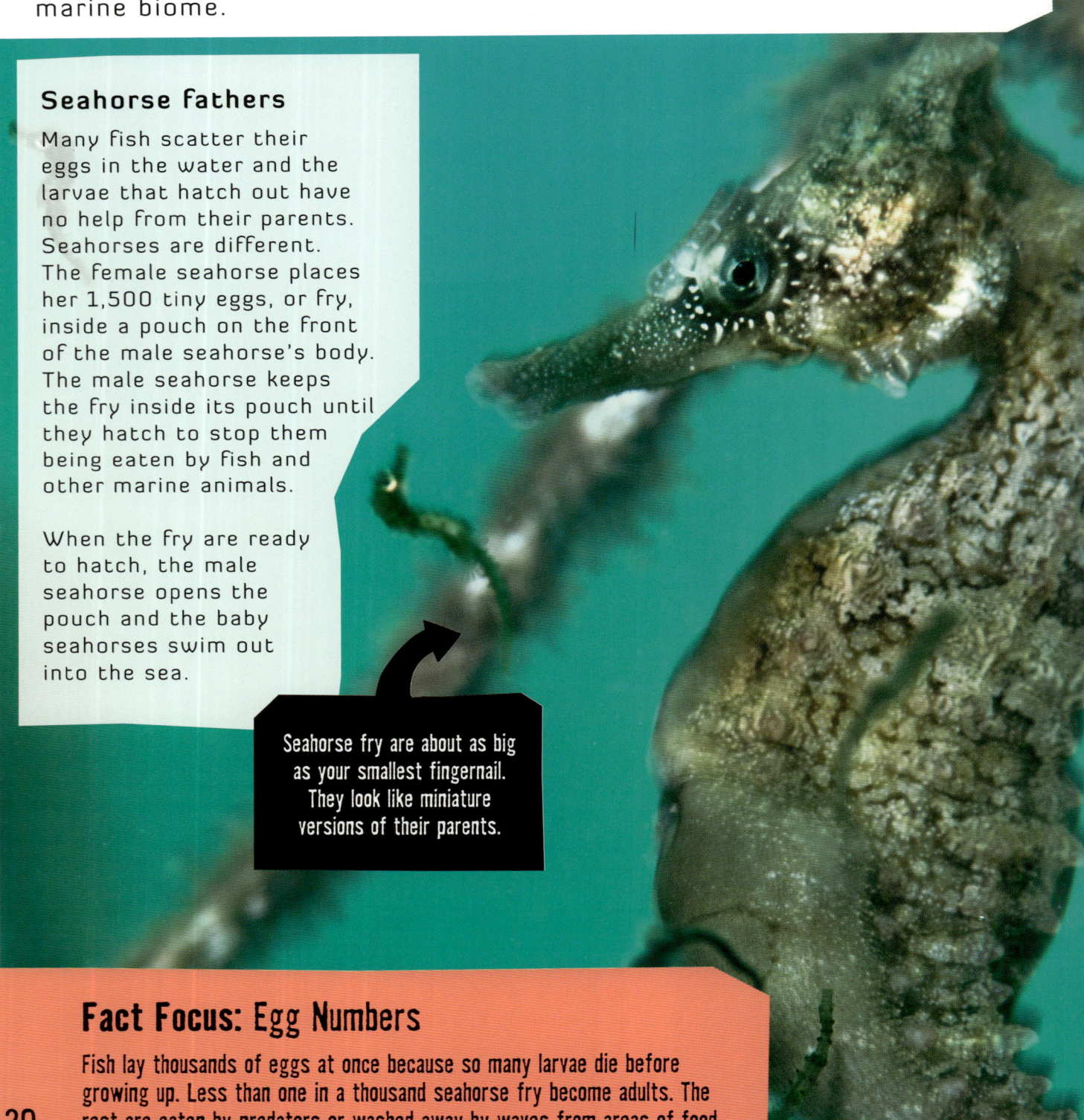

Seahorse fathers

Many fish scatter their eggs in the water and the larvae that hatch out have no help from their parents. Seahorses are different. The female seahorse places her 1,500 tiny eggs, or fry, inside a pouch on the front of the male seahorse's body. The male seahorse keeps the fry inside its pouch until they hatch to stop them being eaten by fish and other marine animals.

When the fry are ready to hatch, the male seahorse opens the pouch and the baby seahorses swim out into the sea.

Seahorse fry are about as big as your smallest fingernail. They look like miniature versions of their parents.

Fact Focus: Egg Numbers

Fish lay thousands of eggs at once because so many larvae die before growing up. Less than one in a thousand seahorse fry become adults. The rest are eaten by predators or washed away by waves from areas of food.

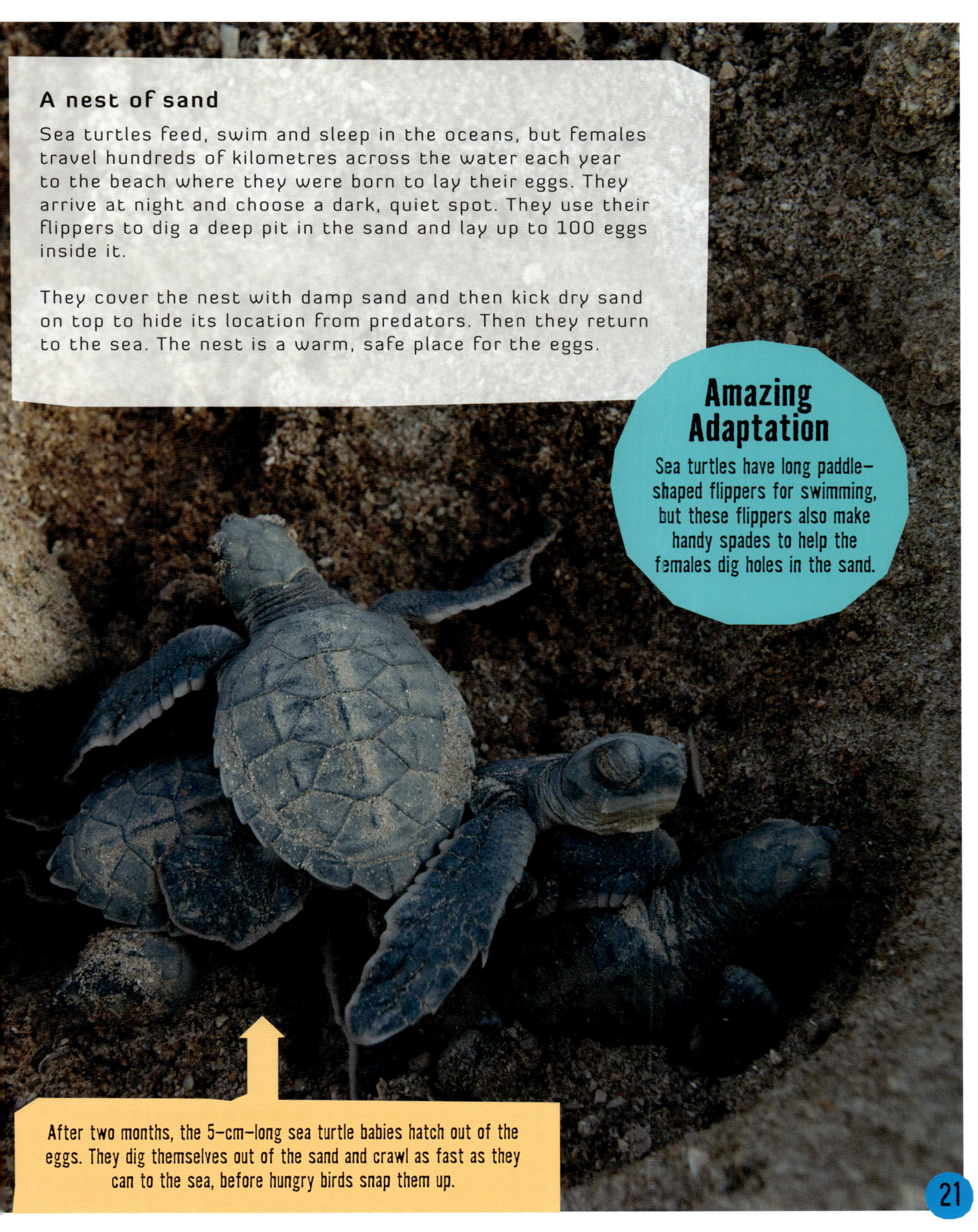

A nest of sand

Sea turtles feed, swim and sleep in the oceans, but females travel hundreds of kilometres across the water each year to the beach where they were born to lay their eggs. They arrive at night and choose a dark, quiet spot. They use their flippers to dig a deep pit in the sand and lay up to 100 eggs inside it.

They cover the nest with damp sand and then kick dry sand on top to hide its location from predators. Then they return to the sea. The nest is a warm, safe place for the eggs.

Amazing Adaptation

Sea turtles have long paddle-shaped flippers for swimming, but these flippers also make handy spades to help the females dig holes in the sand.

After two months, the 5-cm-long sea turtle babies hatch out of the eggs. They dig themselves out of the sand and crawl as fast as they can to the sea, before hungry birds snap them up.

EAT OR BE EATEN

The lives of all marine plants and animals are linked together in different food chains. Food chains tell the story of how food energy is passed from plants to animals.

From phytoplankton to blue whales

Plants are the first link in a food chain as they make their own food using light in the process of photosynthesis. Tiny plants in plankton are called phytoplankton. Phytoplankton are flat and round or have spines or hairs that help them float near the surface to get light.

Phytoplankton are eaten by shrimp-like animals called krill that swim using five pairs of tiny legs. In the Southern Ocean, km-long swarms of krill make easy prey for the next link in that particular food chain: blue whales.

Krill swim towards the surface of the water during the night to look for food and back down into the ocean during the day to try to avoid predators.

Amazing Adaptation

Baleen whales, such as the blue whale, use their tongues to push water through fringed plates inside their mouths that sieve or filter tonnes of krill from the seawater.

From seaweed to sea otters

Some ocean food chains begin with seaweed. Sea snails eat seaweed and are eaten by crabs, which are eaten by seabirds.

Kelp is a type of seaweed eaten by sea urchins. These small, spiky marine animals have a beak-like mouth for grinding up the seaweed. Sea urchins are eaten by sea otters. Sea otters have a wide flat tail they move up and down and webbed feet that help them dive to catch the sea urchins. Their paws have rough pads for grabbing prey.

A sea otter lays on its back at the surface and uses its belly as a dining table while it tucks into its prey. Most sea otters use their paws to break the prickly spines off the sea urchins before they eat them!

Fact Focus: Food Webs

Several food chains together form food webs. For example, the tiny animals in plankton that eat phytoplankton are eaten by mackerel and many other fish, which in turn are eaten by many animals, including seabirds, dolphins and larger fish.

OCEANS AND PEOPLE

All of us depend on the oceans. We travel or carry goods around the world in huge ships and we sail and swim in marine biomes for fun. Oceans and seas also provide us with food, oil, medicines and other substances that we use every day.

From the sea to the shops

Fish and shellfish are an important food source for millions of people and catching, preparing or selling these fish provides millions more with jobs. People also catch krill to make animal feed and use seaweed to make products like ice cream and toothpaste smooth and creamy.

Scuba divers wear oxygen tanks so they can enjoy swimming underwater with amazing marine wildlife like this huge manta ray.

Fact Focus: Overfishing

People are taking more fish out of the ocean than can be replaced by those remaining having young. This means that some, such as Bluefin tuna, are in danger of extinction.

Ocean pharmacies

Marine biomes may not look like your local chemists, but they are an important source of medicines. Scientists make copies of chemicals they find in living things, such as sponges and corals, and use them to develop medicines. Sea squirts have helped to make a cancer medicine and a cone snail has been used to make a painkiller.

The ocean floor

People dig up useful resources from beneath the ocean floor. They drill for oil which is used as a fuel and to make electricity. It's also used to make plastics, fertilisers, fabrics and many other things. Sand and gravel are used in buildings. Metals, such as copper, are used in mobile phones and titanium is used in aircraft.

Sea squirts like this one have been used to make a cancer drug. Sea squirts are so named because they squirt water when removed from the ocean, probably as a form of self-defence!

Fact Focus: Oxygen Supply

The oceans help to give us the air we breathe! Phytoplanktons produce about 70 per cent of Earth's oxygen. They release it as waste when they make their own food by photosynthesis.

MARINE THREATS

Accidentally or on purpose, people dump all sorts of waste in oceans and seas. This pollution puts marine biomes and their wildlife in danger.

Pollution problems

Most marine pollution is solid waste, such as fishing nets and plastic bags. Then there are the dirt and chemicals that are washed down drains from bathrooms or farm fields. Ships sometimes leak or spill oil into oceans when they are damaged.

Oil spills clog fur and feathers, stopping birds and animals from keeping warm. Other animals are injured or killed by rubbish, because they become entangled in it or mistake it for food.

Many sea turtles die each year because they mistake floating plastic bags for the jellyfish they like to eat.

Fact Focus: The Power of Plastic

Plastic floats and takes hundreds of years to rot. Birds starve when their stomachs are full of plastic waste and plastic kills many thousands of other marine animals each year.

Global warming

The gradual rise in world temperatures from global warming is making seas and oceans warmer. Krill need freezing cold water to breed, so there are fewer krill for fish, seals and whales to eat.

Coral polyps share food with the algae that live among them, but algae cannot make food by photosynthesis in very warm water, so they die. This weakens and kills corals, robbing reef animals of the food and shelter they need to survive.

As oceans get warmer, some animals move to parts of the marine biome where it was too cold for them before. Without natural enemies in these places, they are free to devour anything in their path.

Because of the increase in ocean temperatures, thousands of 1-m-wide giant king crabs have invaded the deep Southern Ocean, where they are killing huge numbers of sea urchins, starfish and other wildlife.

MARINE FUTURES

Oceans and seas are beautiful natural biomes full of amazing wildlife and they provide us with many useful resources. It is vital to protect them for the future.

Laws and rules
Many countries have laws to stop people releasing dangerous waste into oceans, about which fish can be caught and where fishing boats can go to prevent overfishing. There are also laws to stop people from hunting or disturbing endangered animals, such as walruses.

Marine reserves
Marine reserves are areas of water protected by law where fishing and mining are banned and the number of people who can visit is limited.

Hawaiian monk seals are an endangered animal, but many now live safely in the Papahānaumokuākea marine reserve.

Fact File: The Papahānaumokuākea Marine National Monument

Location: The Pacific Ocean around the northwestern islands of Hawaii
Size: 1,508,870 km²
Overview: Biggest marine reserve in the world and home to the world's healthiest coral reefs and blue whales, sea turtles and Hawaiian monk seals.

Conservation helps

Some conservation workers rescue injured or ill animals or clean up seabirds after an oil spill. Others study ocean biomes to find out what the problems are and what can be done to help. They inform people about dangers facing marine biomes so that more people get involved in protecting them.

What you can do

You can help marine biomes by reducing waste. Buy reusable items like water bottles and recycle things like cans and mobile phones. Avoid dropping litter, especially at the coast. Look out for opportunities to help on a beach clean-up at a coast near you or when on holiday. You could also support a conservation group that works to protect coasts, oceans and seas.

> Follow the seashore code at the coast. Take care when looking in rock pools. Turn rocks gently and put them back where you found them so you don't destroy animal homes.

Fact Focus: Wind and Wave Power

Burning coal to make electricity is one cause of global warming. In some oceans people build power stations that make electricity using wave or wind power instead of fossil fuels. This reduces the pollution that causes global warming.

GLOSSARY

adaptation special feature or way of behaving that helps a living thing survive in its habitat.

algae plant-like living things that grow in damp places.

bacteria tiny living things that can cause diseases or decompose waste.

biome large region of Earth with living things adapted to the typical climate, soils and other features.

blood vessels tubes inside an animal that carry blood around its body.

blubber thick layer of fat beneath the skin of some animals

breed to have young or babies.

camouflage colours and patterns that help hide an animal's body against its surroundings.

climate typical weather pattern through the year in an area

conservation the act of guarding, protecting or preserving something.

continent one of seven large masses of land: Asia, Africa, North America, South America, Europe, Australia and Antarctica

currents movements of large areas of water in a particular direction

dissolved mixed with a liquid so it becomes part of the liquid.

echolocation way of finding things using echoes that bounce off objects.

endangered at risk of dying out.

Equator imaginary line around the centre of the Earth

extinct when every individual plant or animal of a particular kind has died out.

fertiliser a substance added to soil to help plants grow.

filter to pass something through tiny holes to remove unwanted material.

flippers wide, flat limb (arm or leg) used for swimming.

food chain way of showing animals that eat each other as links in a chain.

food web feeding relationships between living things

fossil fuels natural fuel, such as coal or gas, formed from the remains of living things.

friction the force that makes a moving object slow down when it rubs against another

frond leaf-like parts found on seaweed.

gills body parts that fish and some other animals use to breathe underwater.

global warming rise in average temperature of Earth caused by human use of machines and electricity, which is altering weather patterns worldwide.

habitat place where an animal or plant lives.

holdfast part of a seaweed that anchors it to rocks.

kidneys body parts that remove waste products from the blood.

larvae animals at the stage when they have just hatched out of an egg.

limestone hard sedimentary rock

mollusc animal with a soft body that is usually covered with a shell.

photosynthesis process by which green plants make sugary food using energy in sunlight.

plankton microscopic plants and animals that float in oceans and seas.

pollution something that damages water, air or land or makes it harmful to living things.

predator animal that eats other animals.

prey animal eaten by another animal.

sea level the level of the surface of oceans and seas

seaweed a plant-like living thing found in marine biomes.

streamlined shaped to move more easily through air or water.

tentacles long, flexible animal arms

tide the way the sea moves up and down the shore twice a day.

tropics warm region surrounding the Equator

FIND OUT MORE

Books
Ocean: A Children's Encyclopedia
Dorling Kindersley, 2015

Fast Facts! Ocean Wonders
Kingfisher, 2016

Ultimate Oceanpedia: The Most Complete Ocean Reference Ever
Christina Wilsdon
National Geographic Society, 2016

Earth's Oceans (Where's the Water?)
Peter Castellano
Gareth Stevens Publishing, 2016

Websites
There are games, facts and pictures about oceans at this WWF site:

gowild.wwf.org.uk/oceans

Resources from the organisers of World Ocean Day:

www.worldoceansday.org/splash-bubbles-resources

Find out how to stop ocean pollution at:

www.greenpeace.org/usa/oceans/preventing-plastic-pollution/

INDEX

adaptations 4, 7, 9, 10, 14, 16, 17, 19, 21, 22
animals 4, 5, 8, 9, 11, 12, 14, 15, 16, 17, 18, 19, 20, 22, 23, 26, 27, 28, 29
Australia 13

bacteria 16
biomes 4, 5, 6, 8, 12, 20, 24, 25, 26, 27, 28, 29
birds 5, 11, 21, 26
breathing 5, 8, 14, 25

camouflage 18, 19
climate 5
coastlines 4, 10, 29
conservation 29
continents 6
coral reefs 4, 12, 13
countershading 19

echolocation 17
eggs 20, 21
energy 15, 22
extinction 24

feeding 5, 21
fish 5, 8, 9, 11, 12, 13, 14, 15, 16, 17, 20, 23, 24, 27, 28
food 5, 12, 16, 20, 24, 26, 27
food chains 22, 23
food webs 23

global warming 27, 29

habitat 5, 12
holdfasts 10

ice 6, 14, 15

medicines 25

molluscs 11
moving 9, 15

ocean floor 14, 15, 25
oceans 4, 6, 7, 12, 14, 21, 27, 28, 29
oxygen 8, 24, 25

people 24, 25, 26, 28, 29
photophores 16, 18
photosynthesis 10, 22
plankton 5, 11, 14, 22, 23
plants 4, 5, 14, 22
pollution 26
predators 11, 13, 18, 20, 22
prey 7, 12, 15, 19, 23

resources 25, 28

salt 4, 8
seabed 4
seas 6, 7, 27, 28, 29
seashore code 29
seawater 5, 8, 12, 22
seaweed 5, 8, 10, 23
shells 11
shelter 12, 13, 27
South Africa 4
summer 6, 14
surface 4, 5, 7, 11, 14, 16, 19, 22

teeth 13, 15, 16, 18, 19
tentacles 11, 12, 13, 18

waves 4, 10, 11, 20
winds 4, 10, 11
winter 6

young 5, 20